THE GREAT
HARTFORD
PICTURE BOOK

Wilson H. Faude

This limited edition volume
celebrates the 350th anniversary
of Hartford and the state of
Connecticut.

People's Bank
is proud to present
The Great Hartford Picture Book
in recognition of the
350th Anniversary
of both the
Capital City
and the
State of Connecticut.

With this book
we honor
the citizens of the Hartford area
past, present, and future.

people's bank

THE GREAT
HARTFORD
PICTURE BOOK

from the
Pictorial Archives
of the
Connecticut State Library

by Wilson H. Faude

Associate Compilers:
Mark H. Jones, State Archivist
Theodore O. Wohlsen,
Head: Archives, History and Genealogy Unit

Foreword by
The Honorable William A. O'Neill,
Governor of the State of Connecticut

Introduction by
Clarence Walters,
Connecticut State Librarian

▲
─────────────────────────

This book is gratefully dedicated to
three life-long Hartford residents who
have spent their lives enriching and
contributing to the health and beauty
of our capital city:
Elizabeth Beach Capen,
Mary Wells Edwards,
Robert Hutchins Schutz, Jr.,
and to two very special and
supportive family members:
my sister Ann
and
my wife Janet.

─────────────────────────
▼

The Donning Company/Publishers,
5659 Virginia Beach Boulevard,
Norfolk, Virginia 23502

Edited by Richard A. Horwege

Library of Congress Cataloging-in-Publication Data:

Main entry under title:
The Great Hartford picture book.

  Bibliography: p.
  1. Hartford (Conn.)—History, Pictorial works.
2. Hartford (Conn.)—Description—Views. I. Faude,
Wilson H. II. Jones, Mark H. III. Wohlsen, Theodore O.
IV. Connecticut State Library.
F104.H3G60   1985   974.6′3   85-27424
ISBN 0-89865-450-5

Printed in the United States of America

Contents

Foreword

The people of Connecticut, during 1985 and 1986, are celebrating the 350th anniversary of the founding of our state and the settlement of Hartford, our Capital City.

As a state, we are appropriately characterized as independent Connecticut Yankees who inhabit a land of steady habits. We preserve and we pioneer. Our land is not rich in natural resources, yet our human resources have more than compensated through our ingenuity and inventiveness.

This pictorial collection shares part of Hartford's landscape and is reflective of change seen across our state. The more than 300 images contained in these pages present our people working, parading and building. Many of the then-new facades have now been lost, except on film. Many of the exciting unveilings and parades are distant memories. It is appropriate that we remember and reflect on these images, learn from them, enjoy them, and use them and their lessons confidently as we continue to grow as a state.

As Governor of Connecticut, I am especially proud that some of the vast resources of our State Library are the source for this book. It is very appropriate to showcase our pictorial archives in this, our 350th anniversary year.

I want to extend my appreciation to the author, Wilson H. Faude, the staff of the State Library, and especially to David Carson, President of the People's Bank, who made this anniversary volume possible.

William A. O'Neill
Governor

Preface

This year Hartford and Connecticut celebrate their 350th birthdays. It is both appropriate and exciting that on this occasion this great collection of photographs, exclusively from the State Library's pictorial archives is being published.

The purpose of this book is to share. I have chosen the scrapbook approach in order to allow for the publication of these over 300 photographs, many of which are being published for the first time. These include the buildings by the river that were demolished in the building of the Bulkeley Bridge in 1903 and the images of Mulberry Street that was "absorbed" in the 1960s with the creation of the Bushnell Plaza complex. Some pictures are included simply because they are spectacular, such as the dramatic image of the first train into the city, following the Blizzard of 1888: all snow, with the black smokestack plowing along.

These photographs record and share the changing nature of our city and yet, for all its changes, many remarkable statements of continuity survive. Premier among these are the Butler-McCook Homestead, the Old State House and the Wadsworth Atheneum. All around these landmarks, buildings and streets have come and gone. A select number of buildings remain as marble pillars in an ever-changing sea.

This book is not intended to make the statement that we should preserve everything. I do believe that we should know where we have been, what once happened or stood where, if for no other reason than to be able to evaluate where we are, and perhaps have an inkling of where we are, or are not, going.

These photographs clearly document the evolution that has so clearly affected and changed our city. Founded beside the great Connecticut River, we are currently blocked from its banks by dikes and massive spaghetti loops of highways. Our rolling streets have been corrected into level runs. Our buildings, once corniced with inviting entrances and street level windows, have become sleek impersonal monoliths of protective reflective glass.

There are positive signs resulting in the reevaluation of the highways and impersonal architecture. These have come from concerned citizens who have recognized problems and instead of muttering, have properly organized themselves in order to be able to do something. They range from Sue Connor, Jared Edwards, Ruth and Joe Pagano, Tyler Smith and Sally Weeks who, after the loss of the Loomis-Wooley House, began the discussions that evolved into the Hartford Architecture Conservancy. The conservancy has done so much to raise our consciousness and to preserve so many of our buildings. In the fall of 1975, when the Old State house was threatened with demolition, Stanley Schultz first sounded the alarm, and with the help of Morrison Beach, Elizabeth Capen, Joan Friedland, Bob Smith and so many others, the landmark was saved. Of all the tasks, none seems more herculean than that of again being able to reach our great river. Today, Riverfront Recapture is a vital entity—the brainchild of Rory O'Neil.

This picture book is a beginning. Hopefully those who have photographs of their homes and neighborhoods will consider donating them to our State Library so everyone can enjoy them. I hope this book is merely the beginning of many that recall and share the changing image of Hartford and hopefully other cities throughout the state.

Above all else, this is your book. Read into the photographs, share anecdotes, or stand on the same corner pictured and look back to what was and pause. We can all be justly proud of our heritage, whether we are descendants of the founders of this city or merely spending our first night here. With the exception of the Sukiaugs who originally walked these banks, we are all immigrants. One hopes that in the next 350 years, we will be mindful as we shape and reshape the character and the quality of life of our city.

WILSON H. FAUDE

Acknowledgments

Every book relies on the cooperation and sharing of so many individuals. This book is no exception. We all owe a debt of thanks to Mr. David Carson, President and Mr. Fred Judd of People's Bank for their support of this book. Without it, the project would not have happened.

All of the photographs were carefully reproduced by Gus Johnson of Windsor. Gus worked and reworked many of the early images to achieve the clarity we enjoy here.

Last, and most important, the staff of Connecticut's State Library enthusiastically encouraged this book and gave their counsel and time above and beyond the call of duty. One can be justly proud of these quintessential professionals on the State Librarian Clarence Walter's staff. Two deserve special credit here, simply because without their help this book would not have been possible: Mark Jones, State Archivist; and Ted Wohlsen, Head of the Archives, History and Genealogy Unit. Because of their help, and all the staff's, it is with pleasure that I note that part of the royalties from this book are being donated to the State Library to the photographic division.

Introduction

It is appropriate that *The Great Hartford Picture Book* should appear during the concurrent commemorations of the founding 350 years ago of Connecticut and the City of Hartford. In the book, readers are given a glimpse of the people, homes, shops, streets and events which made up Hartford during the last decades of the nineteenth and first decades of the twentieth centuries. Photographs show a simpler society being transformed into a complex modern society by the forces of industrialization, immigration and war. The opulence of the wealthy existed alongside the poverty of working class and immigrants. Streets vibrated with the hustle and bustle of laborers, children, business-men, housewives, tourists, attorneys, politicians and judges, society women, ethnic and Yankee shopkeepers and deliverymen in animal-drawn and motorized vehicles. Hartford attracted the immigrants and the famous and mighty, such as fighter Jack Dempsey, President Teddy Roosevelt and presidential candidate James G. Blaine. As the seat of state government, the city hosted inaugural processions and mourned at a funeral of one chief executive. During World War I, Hartford served as the head-quarters for the superagency known as the State Council of Defense, as a processing center and disembarkation point for draftees, and as a site for patriotic parades and demonstrations of wartime material, such as gas masks and tanks.

Like other cities, Hartford experienced planned and unplanned changes in its urban landscape, and the book contains photographs of such events as fires at Union Station and St. Joseph's Cathedral, the toppling of the Pearl Street Congregational Church steeple, the Flood of 1936, the last run of the last horse-drawn trolley and the first appearance of the electric trolley—both on the same day.

The photographs in this book were reproduced from originals in the pictorial archives and archival record groups of the Archives, History and Genealogy Unit of the Connecticut State Library. Through this unit the State Library administers and makes available a unique statewide Connecticut local history and genealogy collection, the state archives, a large map collection and the pictorial archives.

The State Library first organized its pictorial collec-tion in 1976-1977 with a grant from the Library Services and Construction Act. For years the State Library had received photographs, posters, post cards, business cards and other similar items. The grant enabled the library to make its pictorial resources available by organizing the eighty-thousand item collection into sixty-three picture groups and publishing the *Guide to Pictorial Archives in the Connecticut State Library.** Significant groups of photo-graphs remaining in archival record groups were identified. As the *Guide* indicates, the pictorial archives is a multi-faceted collection, containing "picture forms which range from miniature cartes de visite to colossal posters, from glass-plate negatives to bookplates, and from vintage pho-tography to mass-produced prints." *The Great Hartford Picture Book* reveals the variety and quality of picture forms available.

Readers will respond in different ways to the portrait of turn-of-the-century Hartford offered in the following pages. While some researchers may be impressed with scenes of buildings and streets, others will find impressive and exciting documentation of daily urban life more than fifty years ago. For this record we are indebted to the literally hundreds of persons, many of whom are unknown, who contributed to the pictorial archives. William Dudley, a commercial photographer located on Main Street who was also associated with the *Hartford Courant*, took photo-graphs of Hartford during the First World War and left the glass-plate negatives of these priceless shots to the State Library. Another benefactor was the Taylor family. Samuel Taylor, president of the State Savings Bank, amassed a large collection of photographs of Hartford and left them to his daughters, Mary and Ada Taylor. Mary Taylor later donated the glass-plate negatives of this collection to the library.

Several photographs of Hartford and the rest of Connecticut remain in archival record groups. This book contains a few examples. An unknown photographer produced stunning documentation of Hartford's immigrant neighborhoods for the Connecticut Woman Suffrage Asso-ciation's anti-vice campaign. Pictorial evidence of one Depression-era public works project—the construction of the Colt Park swimming pool in 1934—is also included. Photographs of this project and others carried out by the Emergency Relief Commission are found in Record Group 32.

It is hoped that *The Great Hartford Picture Book* will inform and entertain. Citizens of Connecticut should benefit in two additional ways. Perhaps the book will spur readers to explore their closets, attics, and bookcases for pictures of Connecticut and will consider donating them to the State Library. Potential donors are encouraged to contact the State Archivist at 566-3690.

Equally important, some of the royalties from the sales of the book will return to the State Library and will be placed in a special fund for the maintenance and preserva-tion of picture forms in the archives so that future generations will also be able to enjoy a glimpse of a society long vanished. During this year of important historical commemorations in Connecticut, it is fitting that *The Great Hartford Picture Book* should educate readers and contribute to the preservation of this unique historical record.

*Copies of the *Guide to Pictorial Archives* are available as long as supplies last. Contact the Archives, History and Genealogy Unit of the Connecticut State Library at 566-3692.)

Clarence R. Walters, State Librarian

Albany Avenue

Albany Avenue is one of Hartford's oldest streets. In the earliest days it was probably an Indian trail, and later used by the early settlers. In 1678 it was laid out as the Talcott Mountain Turnpike, and was popularly called the Albany Road as it was the stage road to Albany. On it were many well known taverns and later many fine houses.

On the corner of Albany and Prospect stood the Wadsworth Tavern. It still stands, thought it has been moved to face Prospect and not Albany as shown here.

The Goodwin Tavern on Albany Avenue was a sizeable establishment with a more than local reputation for its fine food and hospitality. It has since been demolished.

This was the residence of Francis H. Richards at the corner of Albany and Edwards Street.

James Goodwin Batterson's home on Albany Avenue was designed by George Keller. Batterson was a contractor who built the Library of Congress, the capitols of Connecticut and New York, and as a Greek Scholar did his own translations of the *Iliad* and the *Odyssey*. One day, March 24, 1864, to be precise, Batterson met a friend, James Bolter. Bolter knew of Batterson's idea to insure travelers. "How much would you charge to insure me against accident between here and Buckingham Street," Bolter asked. "Two cents," Batterson replied, and the premium was delivered. Bolter made it safely, and on April 1, 1864, Batterson opened The Travelers Insurance Company, to insure travelers from accidents.

Ann & Allyn Streets

This is the corner of Ann and Allyn streets as it looked prior to 1894. The house on the corner has recently suffered a devastating fire, and is still attracting curious spectators. At some point this house and those adjacent were demolished to make a proper site for the Masonic Temple.

Where modern office buildings stand today, once stood homes and gardens and orchards. Ann Street was named by James and Nathaniel Goodwin in honor of their mother, and originally only designated a street they cut through their farmland near Main Street in the early 1800s.

The Masons constructed this great Masonic Temple on the corner of Ann and Allyn streets in 1894. The architect was Books M. Lincoln of Hartford. It is hard to appreciate the full impact of the architecture, now that directly across the street is the Hartford Civic Center and the fact that Allyn Street, which once went through to Trumbull, now stops at Ann.

Ann Street once hosted some of the finest homes in the city. Shown here is the home of Dr. Charles E. Jones at 116 Ann Street.

Asylum Street

Originally laid out as the road from "the Meeting House to the Mill" and eventually on to Litchfield, Asylum Street has always been one of Hartford's busiest streets. Some merchants, such as Stackpole, Moore and Tryon have been on the street for years. Others, such as Huntington's Bookstore can date its direct lineage on Asylum Street back to the early 1800s. This is the land of steady habits.

This is a view of Asylum from Main. Everything from hats to diamonds, books to tintypes, billiards and even a clothing bazaar and hardware could be found on this fertile street.

At the corner of Asylum and Haynes streets stands the Goodwin Building. Built in 1881, following the death of Mr. James Goodwin, it featured commercial space at street level and luxury apartments above. Kimball and Wisedell of New York were the designers, though Mr. Goodwin's son, the Rev. Francis Goodwin, himself an amateur architect and thoroughly knowledgeable in the Queen Anne style, must have guided the design. Today the future of the Goodwin building is in question, especially as developers threaten to build a massive tower on the Pearl Street section and greatly rearrange the original spaces.

On the corner of Trumbull and Asylum stood the Allyn House, once one of the city's most fashionable hotels. The site is now occupied by the Hartford Civic Center. Its architecture is inviting and close to the pedestrian, its shops designed to draw one into the windows and in to purchase. How differently the retailing designers design today. One wonders which is more successful.

The first time a president of the United States rode in an automobile was on May 22, 1902. Theodore Roosevelt was the president and the event occurred in Hartford. Pictured here is President Roosevelt with Col. Jacob L. Green, president of the Connecticut Mutual Life Insurance Company, in Colonel Green's electric car, passing Asylum at Trumbull. There is a side note to this great occasion. Much to President Roosevelt's surprise and dissatisfaction, it was Colonel Green and not the mayor of Hartford who escorted the president. Roosevelt thought he was the guest of the mayor and should have been accompanied by the mayor. Looking at the photograph, and Colonel Green, it may also have been that Colonel Green was not the best of company.

Asylum Street

These children hopped a free ride at the corner of Asylum and Ford streets. The Hotel Garde on Asylum is in the background.

The hill west of Union Station on Asylum Street was popularly called Lord's Hill, probably after Thomas Lord who had a house there. At the foot, for many years stood The Chicken Coop restaurant, where the finest fried chicken in the city could be found. The restaurant closed its doors in August of 1985, and the site was slated for demolition for the highway system.

At the crest of Lord's Hill, where Broad Street now crosses Farmington and Asylum stood the home of Thomas Day. Helen Post Chapman remembered in *My Hartford of the Nineteenth Century* that "the iron dog on the triangle of green lawn was always on the alert. Had he eyes to see and ears to hear how much he might have recounted." The Day house, shown here, stood until 1928 when, following the death of Mrs. Day, the city demolished the house to extend Broad Street. Behind the house can be seen the Netherlands Hotel, which stood until the 1960s.

The triangular site of land is partially preserved as Gallaudet Square, dedicated in 1932 in honor of Thomas Hopkins Gallaudet, the educator of the deaf whose school was across the street where The Hartford now has its corporate headquarters. On Gallaudet Square is the statue by Francis Wadsworth commemorating the founders of the school for the deaf, and featuring little Alice Cogswell in a pair of hands.

Many visitors find it curious that one of Hartford's principle streets is named Asylum, presumably after an insane asylum. In fact, Asylum Street and Avenue were named out of a sense of pride for the first school for the education of the deaf in America: The Asylum for the Deaf and Dumb, which was located on Asylum Avenue at the crest of Lord's Hill.

The story of the founding of this school in Hartford is worth sharing here. Dr. Mason Fitch Cogswell was a distinguished Hartford physician whose daughter Alice lost her hearing as a result of brain fever at the age of two. Thomas Gallaudet, son of the family next door and a divinity student at Andover, spent some time with Alice and made remarkable progress in teaching her. Dr. Cogswell and others raised funds to send Gallaudet to Europe to study. On his return in 1817, with Laurent Clerc, he opened the school now known as the American School for the Deaf. In 1819, with proceeds alloted by Congress, the school purchased the site on Lord's Hill and built the school. The building and site were sold to The Hartford in 1919, and in 1921 the school moved to West Hartford.

In front of the building is the bust of Laurent Clerc (1785-1869), the distinguished teacher of the deaf. It is preserved on the West Hartford campus.

Asylum Avenue developed into a premier residential street. Pictured here is the home of George L. Chase at 914 Asylum Avenue.

19

Asylum Street

The first Catlin Building at the corner of Main and Asylum streets is seen here. In 1957 Burt's Shoe Store stood at this location. Huntsinger's Business College was at 30 Asylum Street.

At the corner of Main and Asylum stands Hartford's first skyscraper. It was built in 1912 by the Hartford-Aetna Realty Corporation. Designed by Donn Barber of New York, it has suffered over the years from aluminum and chrome improvements, but still stands elegant and proud.

This is the Catlin Block as it looked in the eary 1920s.

Blizzard of 1888

On Sunday night, March 11, 1888, a light snow began to fall and then ended about midnight on Monday the 12th. Then it began to snow again and kept on snowing...and snowing...and snowing. When it finally stopped, Hartford had over thirty-six inches of snow. Some parts of New England recorded as much as fifty inches.

Mulberry Street once ran from Bushnell Park to the Wadsworth Atheneum on Main Street. It was absorbed by the creation of the Bushnell Plaza Complex in the 1960s. Today, John Chapin's Shenanigans Restaurant stands on the site of Mulberry Street. Looking toward the Atheneum, the snow of the blizzard is piled in the street so at least pedestrians could walk on the sidewalks. The merchant on the left is advertising "Wines, Liquor and Lager Beer," while on the right, "8 Bowling Alleys" are an attraction.

The sidewalk beside the Old State House on Central Row is cleared of snow, looking toward the American Hotel.

Asylum Street, looking west from Main, is shown awaiting the removal of snow from the street.

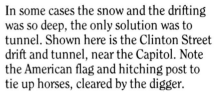

In some cases the snow and the drifting was so deep, the only solution was to tunnel. Shown here is the Clinton Street drift and tunnel, near the Capitol. Note the American flag and hitching post to tie up horses, cleared by the digger.

Many residents were completely snowed in, including William H. Lockwood, whose home is shown here. It was weeks before the city got back to normal.

Blizzard of 1888

On State Street, outside the U.S. Hotel someone, in jest, hung an effigy titled: "The Author of Beautiful Snow." Despite the disaster, a sense of humor survived. Note the little dog at the second floor window being held to watch the crowd.

Then as now, what to do with snow is a city problem. In the Blizzard of 1888, the snow was dumped at the foot of Trumball Street. In the background is the steeple of Center Church.

Isolated for days, it was great news when the first train of the Connecticut Western Railroad made it through to Hartford.

The AUTHOR of Beautiful Snow

Early Bridges

As early as 1809 Hartford had bridges crossing the Connecticut River. This great wooden bridge was built in 1818, and when trolleys came along, it was strong and wide enough to accommodate them as well as horse-drawn vehicles. Note the entrance sign:

"Walk your horses," and beside it the advertising opportunity:

"To see the bargains in Mulcahy's window."

The old wooden bridge burned in a spectacular fire in 1895. This modern picture appears to be the morning after, with the old bridge still smoldering, and the ever-curious paying their last respects.

Ferry service was returned to the river after the old bridge burned, and then a temporary bridge of steel was erected. Debate over what kind of bridge to build went on for years. Finally, in 1902, at the urging of the Board of Trade and Businessman's Association, it was voted to build a new permanent bridge of stone. The bridge was to be called the City Bridge, but later was named in honor of Morgan G. Bulkeley, who served as chairman of the Bridge Commission. Bulkeley was a remarkable person. He served as mayor of Hartford and governor of Connecticut. He was the first president of Baseball's National League and is in the Baseball Hall of Fame. He also saved the Old State House from demolition in 1915. Most people mispronounce his name. It is not Buck-eley, but Bul-keley, as in Bull Kelley.

The removal of the old bridge piers was photographed on November 9, 1903. Though work proceeded on the new stone bridge, for three years debate raged in the courts as some wanted it to be a drawbridge to aid commerce up river. In the background can be seen the pitched tower of the Cheney Building, now The Richardson, on Main Street.

Early Bridges

This is the temporary bridge looking toward Hartford, September 11, 1903.

In the middle of the river stood Dayton Island. This photograph was taken by William H. Thompson, a professional photographer, on November 19, 1905. Thompson's collection is at the State Library complete with glass negatives.

The Hartford Dredging Company's
steam-shovel barge was photographed
on November 13, 1903, dredging the
river in preparation for building the piers
for the new stone bridge.

Building the Bulkeley Bridge

As part of the work for the new bridge, photographers were to record not only the actual construction of the bridge, but also the surrounding landscape, and even the buildings that would be razed for the new great Connecticut Boulevard. This picture, taken on October 24, 1903 shows the view from the new bridge, looking north to Riverside Park.

Even today Riverside Park is an unsung jewel in Hartford. Thanks to Riverfront Recapture, attention is at last being paid to the greatest of our natural resources, the Connecticut River, and the open spaces that we managed not to cover with asphalt or highways. Reaching the river is being led by a few pioneering citizens, yet it will be due to each of us, with our desire to clean up, to lobby, and to contribute, that the concrete of the forties, fifties, and sixties will be put in its proper place. The greatest and perhaps most rewarding membership for all who read this book is to give sweat, blood, and cash to Riverfront Recapture, that the Algonquin "Connecticut," beside the great tidal river, may again be relevant for us, and those who follow.

For the new bridge, it was necessary to extend the riverbank eastward. This picture, taken November 27, 1903, is simply titled: "Making land, north of the bridge, with dredgings."

One of the piers for the Bulkeley Bridge is shown under construction on July 26, 1904.

The River House, which stood just north of the foot of State Street, was photographed on April 10, 1905. One is conscious of the easy access to the river. In the upper right can be seen the piers and the construction for the new stone bridge.

Building the Bulkeley Bridge

Before the stone for the arch was cut, an exact templet was made. Shown here is one of the templets, spread out in a warehouse on September 22, 1904. The numbers were transferred to each stone, so when lifting the massive stones into place, each would fit as it should, and the arch and the bridge would stand.

With meticulous care, each stone in the arch was set as shown on July 14, 1905. The wooden support was removed once the arch was keyed.

Three of the eastern arches on the Bulkeley Bridge were keyed on November 1, 1905.

Building the Bulkeley Bridge

As part of the construction of the new bridge, Connecticut Boulevard was created. It ran north of State Street, to Morgan, and then across the Bulkeley Bridge. One of the blocks razed to provide this great avenue was the Pallotti Block. Some of the city's earliest buildings were there. The back yard of the Pallotti Block is seen here. Note the poster advertizing the Hartford Opera House, "3 nights, 3 matinees, Commencing November 19 (1906) *The Shadow Behind the Throne.*" To the far right a man in a black coat holds a surveyor's pole, indicating the new grade level of the great boulevard yet to be constructed.

Pallotti Block's east end was photographed November 23, 1906. Again the Hartford Opera House's advertising is preeminent with the forthcoming show *The Cow Puncher.* The new grade for the boulevard would be at the top of the billboard.

This old stone building was at the corner of Ferry and Commerce streets. The surveyor indicates the new level of the grade required for Connecticut Boulevard on September 10, 1906. The side advertising disks note "Cigars, 5¢."

Bridge Week 1908

In celebration of the completion of the Bulkeley Bridge, Hartford hosted an extravaganza called "Bridge Week." Parades, concerts, costume events, and more parades highlighted this great occasion which ran from October 6th through the 8th, 1908.

From a rooftop at the corner of Pearl and Main, spectators look down Main at one of the parades. Note all the bunting.

No proper parade is complete without floats, and the Hartford Bridge Week parades had plenty of floats, of all sizes, for every group possible. The Cushman Chuck Company's float (today Cushman Industries) displays their standard: "One Days Production."

The Billings and Spencer Company's float shows their Pyramid "B."

The Billings and Spencer Company had a vast complex on Broad Street. Once threatened with demolition, the complex has been converted into apartments, signaling the return to the city of readaptive living spaces.

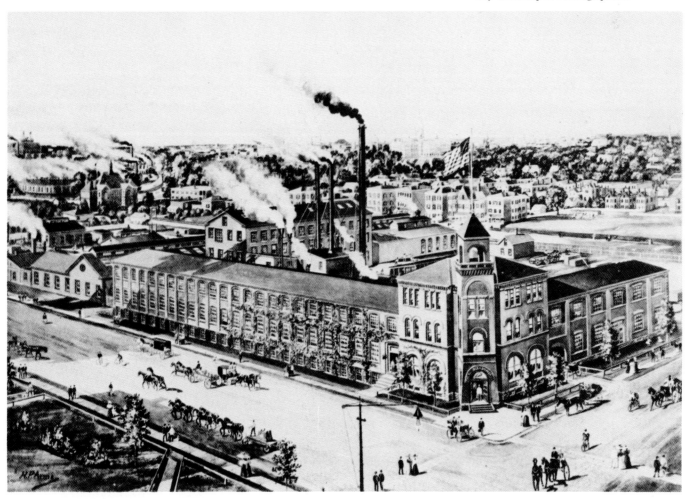

Bridge Week 1908

Pope Manufacturing Company was the manufacturer of the automobile and the bicycle "Columbia."

MOTOR CARRIAGE FACTORY.   COLUMBIA BICYCLE FACTORIES.   HARTFORD CYCLE WORKS.

POPE MANUFACTURING CO., HARTFORD, CONN.

In tribute to the early great navigators and explorers of America, Vikings showed up for the parade.

"Flora" was drawn by white horses, complete with spider web at the rear.

The Putnam Phalanx marched proudly on the new Connecticut Boulevard. Colt's Dome can be seen in the background.

Bridge Week 1908

Everyone participated in Bridge Week, either as a marcher or as a watcher.

There was an elaborate pageant opening Bridge Week on Tuesday, October 6, 1908, of the likes Hartford probably will never see again. On the East Hartford Hartford side, a group of Hartford residents assembled in Puritan costume representing the Rev. Thomas Hooker and his congregation. True to the script the correct number of cattle and sheep and oxen were with them and Mrs. Hooker was carried on a litter. At the appointed signal, others dressed as Indians canoed out to greet the party. Reverend Hooker and his flock were then transported by ferry across the Connecticut, and refounded Hartford. The Indians assembled along the Hartford side of the river, awaiting the Rev. Thomas Hooker on the opposite bank.

Horses, oxen, and household goods were
all part of the pageant. Note the portable
spinning wheel.

Bridge Week 1908

With the actual pageant over, the participants began to mingle, and afforded photo opportunities.

Prominent buildings were illuminated as part of Bridge Week. Here the Old State House, then City Hall, is picked out with light bulbs, including Justice and her scales.

The Hon. Morgan G. Bulkeley in his top hat and mason's regalia supervised the laying of the last stone on the bridge that would bear his name on Thursday, October 8, 1908, 10:30 a.m. It is the largest stone arched bridge in the world: 82 feet wide and 1,193 feet long. Designed by Edwin D. Graves, and built over seventy years ago, today it is part of Interstate 84.

The completed Bulkeley Bridge was photographed on October 11, 1908. The great road that sweeps to the right is the new Connecticut Boulevard.

Bridge Week 1908

This view of the Bulkeley Bridge is from the East Hartford shore with the skyline of Hartford.

Bushnell Park

The land beside the Park River was occupied by factories, slums, and other questionable structures. After years of agitation and hard work, primarily led by the Rev. Horace Bushnell, in 1853 the citizens of Hartford voted to appropriate funds for the establishment of a park in the center of the city. This meant the purchasing of the land and the tenements beside the river, razing the structures and creating what was then called City Park. This was the first park in the world that was created by a city. Previously, parks were merely comprised of undeveloped land.

The Rev. Horace Bushnell had not endeared himself to many in his fight to rid the city of the slums and to create the park. However, three days before his death, on February 14, 1876, the Common Council voted to change the name to Bushnell Park in his honor.

This is the eastern entrance to the park, crossing the Park River, looking toward Trinity College. The campus occupied the site adjacent to the park from 1823 until 1872. The site was then purchased by the city for the new state capitol building for the sum of $500,000.

The campus of Trinity College was atop Bushnell Park (1823-1872). Helen Post Chapman described the campus in *My Hartford of the Nineteenth Century* as: "surrounded by beautiful trees and in their shade grew the bluest, longest stemmed violets that I have ever picked. Trinity College commencement was very imposing. Headed by the president, the faculty and the trustees, the students walked across Bushnell Park to Christ Church for the ceremony, the senior class in cap and gown."

Trinity's new campus on Summit Street was designed by William Burges. The long walk was but one small part of a great master plan. The Trustees of Trinity hired F.H. Kimball to super-intend the actual construction. On July 1, 1875, Bishop John William broke ground, and nearly three years later classes began at the new campus.

Bushnell Park

The corner of Trinity Street and Elm Street is shown here when it was all residential.

Looking up Elm Street from the park, one can see the new State Capitol Building which was designed by Richard UpJohn. The state held its first legislative session there on March 26, 1878.

This view of Bushnell Park shows the Soldiers and Sailors Memorial Arch and the Capitol Building. This is the view of the front side of the capitol; the back side faces Capitol Avenue.

The arch was Connecticut's monument to those who served in the Civil War, and is the first triumphal arch erected in America. It was designed by George Keller and erected in 1885. The ashes of the architect and his wife are interred there. Atop the towers, one can see the terra cotta angels trumpeting victory. These were later removed due to decay and lightning. Today the restoration of the arch is a major project of the Bushnell Park Foundation, the group that has done so much to restore and replant this great park.

Across from the arch, at the corner of Pearl and Ford streets stood the Y.M.C.A. Designed by Edward T. Hapgood to complement Keller's arch, its demolition in the 1970s was a great loss to the city. Today its site serves as an asphalt parking lot.

Bushnell Park

Bushnell park is seen here in the early spring. The Park River was put underground following the Flood of 1936 and the Hurricane of 1938.

On October 15, 1897, the Park Board accepted the gift of a fountain from John J. Corning of New York in memory of his father, Mr. John B. Corning of Hartford. The fountain was designed and sculpted by J. Massey Rind of New York and the fountain was formally accepted on November 24, 1899. To many it is the favorite landmark in Bushnell Park. At the top, a hart is about to leap across a river, fording a play on the capitol's name. Below is a group of Indian maidens, standing in a growth of corn. The maidens are seven feet in height. At the base are four Indian chiefs: one hunting, one at war, one wise, and one watchful. The fountain was in disrepair for many years, but has now been fully restored thanks to the Bushnell Park Foundation.

These photographs are simply labeled:
"July 4th Pageant at Bushnell Park—
Miss Moran."

Bushnell Park

The foot bridge over the Park River in Bushnell Park is seen here. Just beyond the bridge one can see the railroad tracks, headed for Union Station, which is out of camera range, but on the right.

Center Church & Gold Street

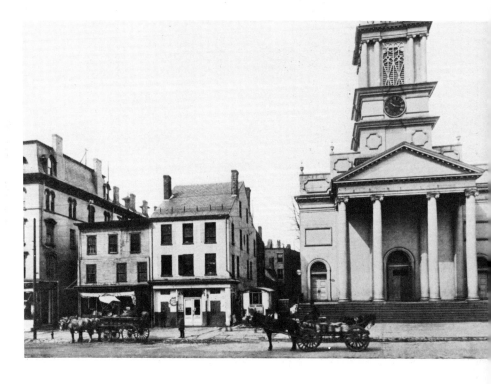

Center Church is Hartford's Rev. Thomas Hooker's Church. In 1807 the parish built this fine edifice, believed to have been designed by Daniel Wadsworth. To the left of the Church is a small alley, Gold Street, then called Factory Lane. It led from Main street to the factories that lined the Park River. To the far left is the City Hotel which was built in 1819.

In 1900, Emily Seymour Goodwin Holcomb led the drive to clean up Gold Street and to preserve the old burial ground. Under her incredible leadership the street was cleared of buildings and a wonderful wrought iron fence was erected beside the site. Today the burial ground is again a matter of concern and is properly receiving the attention of many residents. Organized as the Old Burial Ground Association, funds are being raised for the preservation and restoration of this special site. Note the Jewell Belting factory in the background at the corner of Trumbull and Jewell streets, and in the far distance the tower of the Hartford Public High School.

In the 1960s, in creating Bushnell Plaza, the lines of Gold Street were shifted to the south, and Mulberry Street was absorbed.

In shifting Gold Street, a wonderful triangular plot was created. In 1977 as a gift from the Hartford Foundation of Public Giving, Carl Andre's "Field Stone Sculpture" was erected. So much has been made of this creation, and unfortunately the foundation has taken the blame. To set the record straight, the foundation, in honor of its fiftieth anniversary, presented the city of Hartford with some funds for the creation of a public sculpture. The city then matched these funds with monies from the National Endowment and enlisted the artist, Carl Andre. Some condemn, others love these boulders. They are a dramatic foil and yet complement the old burial ground and Pei's very ordered Bushnell Tower.

On April 1, 1985, Attorney Robert Basine sent to the city a bill on behalf of his client, an unknown sculptor, who had added a row of little rocks, or rockettes, to the original. Shown here is the last of these spinoffs; The Courant carried the story on the front page. Many told Basine he was lucky that no one had hurled his client's addition through a window, or sued for desecration of art. Too many forgot to check the date.

Just south of Gold street stood the City Hotel. It was the premier hotel in Hartford in the nineteenth century. Charles Dickens celebrated his thirtieth birthday here in 1842, and Lafayette and Jefferson Davis dined here. Later it would become, as shown here, the establishment of Linus T. Fenn, purveyor of all things in the home furnishings department. Among his clients were Mark Twain. One cannot doubt Fenn's skill in advertising, as he has literally upholstered the north side of the building with his goods listing.

Center Church & Gold Street

This is the restored graveyard behind Center Church as it looked at the turn of the century, when the church was still painted.

The graveyard today is surrounded by mostly modern buildings.

Looking down Main Street to the south, Center Church stands supreme. The new Metropolitan District Commission building is beyond.

Beside Center Church on Main, one is afforded this view, with the Old State House beyond. Those were the days one could park on Main Street.

Central Row

The Hartford Trust Company, pictured here at the corner of Central Row and Main, was razed so the 1921 Hartford Connecticut Trust Building could dominate the corner. It is clearly sale week on the corner, with the building advertising paint, hosiery and shoe sales.

This view is looking down Central Row to American Row from Main Street. The second building down from the right, the Advest Building, built around 1860, is the lone survivor.

Looking west on Central Row, the Post Office and Old State House are on the right, the Hartford National Bank ahead, and the Central Row block on the left.

Charles Street

Many Hartford streets were eliminated in the 1944 dike improvement plan. Among them was Charles Street, shown here at the corner of Kilbourne. Charles Street was named for the cooper Charles Weeks whose shop was here. A cooper is a tender of barrels. It was a vital skilled profession in early times. John Alden of *Mayflower* and Priscilla fame was a cooper.

Charter Oak

"Welcome to the City of Hartford, the home of the Charter Oak, of which half the town is built." So wrote Hartford resident, Mark Twain. The tree was indeed a heroic specimen White Oak, *Quercus Alba*. In the earliest days, it served as a council tree for the Indians. Connecticut received its charter from Charles II on October 9, 1662, and that document was the legal basis for all its governance. With the accession of James II to the throne, there was the desire to seize the charter. In 1687, Governor Andros arrived in Hartford to collect the Connecticut Charter. A meeting was held, the charter was brought forth, candles went out, and in the dark the charter disappeared. Capt. Joseph Wadsworth had seized the charter and hid it in the great oak which stood on the Wyllys estate, just south of Prospect Street. In a great storm August 21, 1856, the Charter Oak fell.

In 1905 the Society of Colonial Wars erected this monument to the Charter Oak at the corner of Charter Oak Avenue and Place.

Charter Oak

Near the monument, on Charter Oak Avenue, is the Charter Oak Temple. Built in 1876 for the Congregation Beth Israel, it was designed by George Keller and was the first synagogue in the state of Connecticut. In 1982 the preservation and the restoration of the Temple began, and today the building serves as a museum and cultural center for the entire Hartford community. It is preserved by the Charter Oak Temple Restoration Association, COTRA, which has done a valiant job in preserving the landmark.

Charter Oak Place was one of the most fashionable sections of Hartford from the earliest days.

This is the home of Gideon Welles. He was editor and part owner of the *Hartford Evening Press* (1856). Welles was elected to the Connecticut legislature (1827-1835), and later served as secretary of the navy under Lincoln and Johnson (1861-1869).

This home on Charter Oak belonged to Dr. Richard Jordan Gatling (1818-1903), inventor of the famous Gatling gun (1866), a machine gun with six barrels arranged in a circle. It was the first machine gun to be used by the United States Army, and was produced by the Colt factory in Hartford. Dr. Gatling was a medical school graduate, but he never practiced medicine. He spent his life as an inventor.

This is Judge Nathaniel Shipman's house on Charter Oak. The paneling in the library was said to have come from the Charter Oak.

"Uncle Sam" Shipman's "Tavern Group" was an informal gathering patronized by members of Hartford's legal profession. They gathered for suppers of game, oysters, and Connecticut River shad. On one such outing the camera was invited. Standing left to right are: Chauncey Howard, state comptroller; Charles Johnson, clerk of the court; Richard Hubbard, governor (1877-79); and William Eaton, United States senator. Left to right, seated are: Nathaniel Shipman, judge; unidentified servant; William Hammersley, judge, state supreme court; and the host, "Uncle Sam."

Christ Church Cathedral

The tower of Christ Church Cathedral is visible in the background on Main Street looking north.

On the corner is Christ Church Cathedral, in this modern view looking south on Main Street. Designed by Ithiel Town of New Haven in 1828, additions were later designed by Frederick C. Withers and George Keller, and Ralph Adams Cram.

Colonel Samuel Colt

"God created man equal, but Sam Colt made them so." So ran an old expression, in tribute to Col. Sam Colt and his equalizer, the Colt Revolver. Colt was a Hartford boy. His father married well, then committed the unpardonable Yankee sin of dipping into principal and died in bankruptcy. When a boy, Sam went to sea and there conceived of the locking cylinder for the revolver. At a memorial erected to Colonel Colt by his widow, the sailor boy statue is front and center, whittling the beginning of a great fortune. The statue was by James Massey Rhind.

Samuel Colt (1814-1862), built his great home Armsmear on Wethersfield Avenue and under the will of his widow, it still stands as a home for the widows of Episcopal clergymen. The entrance to the home, designed by Octavius Jordan, was through the arch at the far left. The Wethersfield Avenue facade was the rear facade. Stone dogs then and now guard the entrance. The establishment grew pineapples, strawberries, almost any delicacy, including grapes, off season.

Colonel Samuel Colt

Near the Connecticut River, Sam Colt built his great factory, complete with its blue onion dome and gold stars. Many have speculated that it was the gift of a Russian tzar or of a Turkish sultan. Having seen no substantial documentation of either case, the dome is more likely pure advertising of which only a Colt or P. T. Barnum would be capable. Coming to Hartford by river, one would round the bend and gasp: "What's that?" "Colt's factory" would be the answer.

The north wing of Colt's Factory is seen under construction.

Mrs. Colt, one of the greatest hostesses Hartford has ever known, and premier in thoughtful philanthropy, willed the bulk of the Colt estate to the city for public use.

As part of the WPA, a swimming pool was constructed in the Colt Park. An early stage of construction was photographed on October 8, 1934.

The pool was open and a splashing success in 1937.

Connecticut State Library

In 1903, the state legislature authorized the building of a structure to house a state library, a history museum and the state supreme court. All three had outgrown their spaces in the State Capitol and the legislators themselves needed more space. Construction began in 1908 with the digging by shovels and picks for the foundation. All that today is done by machine was laboriously then done by hand with horses to haul away the dirt and stones.

On May 25, 1909, the cornerstone of the Connecticut State Library was set in an official ceremony. The gentlemen in the background are masons in their ceremonial aprons.

This view of the Connecticut State Library under construction is seen from the State Capitol across the street. The architect for the building was Donn Barber of New York with Edward T. Hapgood of Hartford. The building was completed in 1910.

This sunken garden is seen looking out the east entrance of the library, across Washington Street. Today the view is dramatically changed as the neat buildings have been replaced by the 1930-31 State Office Building designed by Smith and Bassette of Hartford.

Early Drugstores

Mr. Charles Allen, left, and Mr. H.H. Wallace, right, stand in the doorway of Marwick Drugstore circa 1908.

Loeffler's Drug Store on Main Street was a Hartford landmark. We do not know who all the people posing here are, or what the occasion was. The last two on the right are H. Howard and H.H. Wallace. The date is 1896.

Mr. H.H. Wallace thought so highly of
the exterior picture, that he went inside
and posed again. He is the one on the
right. This is a special photograph, as it
presents the interior of a turn-of-the-
century drug store. Note the potions and
boxes stacked on the shelves, and the
stencilled decorations.

Farmington Avenue

Farmington Avenue was primarily residential until the Aetna moved to the former Beach-Cooley properties in 1929-31. The home office was designed by James Gamble Rogers. This view shows the Aetna, and beyond, the great highway system that has carved up the area.

At the corner of Farmington Avenue and Laurel Street stood the home of William Braddock Clark, president of the Aetna. The site of the house is today the AFL-CIO building. The house next door survives, though its porch is missing and it has a more modern front.

Saint Joseph's Cathedral was built on Farmington Avenue, across from the site of the Aetna, and was consecrated on May 8, 1892. The great Gothic church served as the seat of the Hartford Diocese, with its marble and onyx altars and great stained glass windows.

On December 31, 1956, the Cathedral of Saint Joseph caught fire. Arson was suspected. To most residents it was amazing that a church of stone could burn so quickly and completely.

Farmington Avenue

This is the home of the Hon. Patrick Garvan at 236 Farmington as it looked in 1900. The house was torn down in 1932.

Mark Twain (Samuel L. Clemens) built this splendid house on Farmington Avenue in 1874. Edward T. Potter was the architect. It was during Twain's Hartford period (1874-1891) that he wrote *The Adventures of Tom Sawyer* (1876), *The Prince and the Pauper* (1881), *Life on the Mississippi* (1883), *Adventures of Huckleberry Finn* (1885), and *A Connecticut Yankee in King Arthur's Court* (1889).

Why did Twain come to Hartford in the first place? His publisher, Elisha Bliss of the American Publishing Company, was here. Also, friends and literary associates such as John and Isabella Hooker and Harriet Beecher Stowe lived here, in the very neighborhood where Twain built his house. Both the Mark Twain and the Harriet Beecher Stowe houses have been restored and are open to the public.

This was the Boardman residence on Farmington Avenue.

This view shows Farmington Avenue looking west in 1889. On the left is Sisson Avenue. So much of the area we think of today as gas stations and fast food was still open country only one hundred years ago.

Ferry Street

Another street greatly absorbed through the years is Ferry Street, which originally ran from Front Street to the river. Seen here are the foundry of M.W. Chapin, one of the Old West Indian Storehouses at the foot of Ferry Street, and the wharf bridge.

This building was at the southwest corner of Ferry Street and Commerce. The sign advertises cash paid for rags, rubber, and metals.

These buildings, including the Riverside Machine Works, were on the north side of Ferry Street, looking east, on November 12, 1905.

This view of Commerce Street, looking north toward the corner of Ferry Street, was taken on April 1, 1906. The billboards advertise the forth-coming attraction, *The Two Johns*. The boat and its ever watchful owner to the right, seem well prepared for the next spring flood.

The Flood of 1936

The winter of 1936 produced unprece-
dented snow falls. In the second week of
March a spring thaw hit New England,
melting the mountains of snow that had
accumulated, filling the Connecticut
River and its tributaries. On March 19,
1936, the high water mark of 29.8 feet,
set in the 1854 flood, was surpassed. The
Flood of 1936 was the most destructive
in the city's history. Amazingly, only five
lives were lost, despite the fact that over
35 million dollars in damage was
incurred. Bushnell Park and Pulalski
Circle became a lake.

These men are travelling down Trumbull
Street by boat. Hicks Street is on the
right, and the phone company building
beyond.

In the lake that shouldn't be, the phone company building shimmers, as if the architect planned it that way.

A young boy makes the flood disaster an adventure in this scene north from Bushnell Park, toward Asylum.

Canoeists paddle toward the Hotel Bond, now DeSales Hall, on Asylum Street, at the intersection of Ann. The hotel had two feet of water in its lobby.

The waters were receding on Front Street. Hoses have been put out to drain basements, so the mop-up could begin.

Front Street

On the earliest maps of Hartford, one sees the "Little River to the North Meadows." East of Main, this river-oriented street later was affectionately known as Front Street. Some of Hartford's earliest surviving buildings and one of its great ethnic neighborhoods was wiped out or transplanted with the decision of the urban renewers to transform the city. Constitution Plaza is the clearest landmark of their efforts at a commercial-retail development. Though it won a lot of awards for design, the plaza as a people space has not worked. Some wish we still had Front Street, with all its personal foibles and real character. Today the street is called Columbus Boulevard, with its location shifted and widened.

This is Front Street, looking north from Ferry, on April 8, 1906. Charles Kramer's store displays new and second hand clothing on the left. Next door the sign offers: "Lodgings—Single Bed," a great improvement over multiple sleeping. On the right, children gather by the door of Rock Teroux's bar.

A group of boys have carefully lined up to please the photographer on Front Street, looking north of Temple, on April 1, 1906.

Many of the old buildings on Front Street had been private homes. Preserved here are the doorways of two: W.L. Wright's house on the left and O.P. Treat's house on the right.

The High School

The Hartford Public High School stood on Hopkins Street. It was designed in 1883 by George Keller, and was a great landmark for years. The football field was next to Farmington Avenue, and many days one could drive by, watching the teams playing in what appeared to be a sea of mud. The building was razed to provide for I-84.

Horse-Drawn Trolley

The last horse-drawn trolley in Hartford is seen here. On May 12, 1895, at 8:48 A.M. the horse-drawn trolley made its final run. On the left, at the corner of Main and State streets the first mechanically-driven trolley can be seen waiting to go into full service. On the right, where the # is, marks the Hon. Henry C. Robinson, former mayor of Hartford. Robinson was a distinguished individual, and greatly respected. President Cleveland asked Robinson to serve as his ambassador to Mexico. Robinson declined. When asked why he declined the position, Robinson simply answered: "What, and leave Hartford?"

Hudson Street

The Old People's Home stood at 20 Hudson Street.

The original Hartford Hospital stood on South Hudson Street.

Before the days of automatic refrigeration, the iceman was essential to the healthy life of any city. Here a Hartford iceman is weighing the ice before delivering it. Children usualy flocked around the iceman hoping for a cool chip of ice to suck on. The wagon bears the quality slogan "Hygeia Ice."

Kilbourne Street

The crowd seen here has presumably gathered to have its picture taken in this view of Kilbourne Street, west from Valley, on November 19, 1905.

The Kilbourne Cafe boasts imported and domestic ales, and next door D. Cohn advertises his blacksmith shop and horse shoeing, on Kilbourne Street, looking east of Front Street on November 19, 1905.

Kinsley Street in Hartford was named for Dr. Apollos Kinsley whose house, the small one in the center, stood there. Kinsley, a prominent inventor, created a machine to make uniform bricks (his 1797 house was built of them), a steam road wagon, and other improvements.

Kinsley Street is the most recent of Hartford's streets to be absorbed.

Sculpting Colonel Knowlton

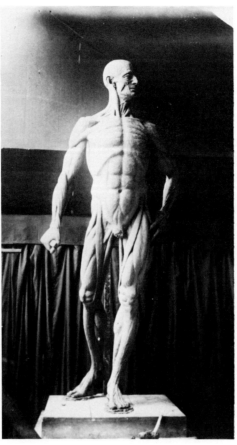

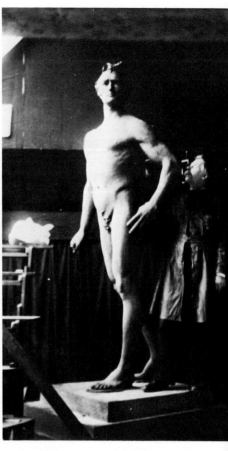

The sculptor made several small versions of the statue, in the flesh and in uniform, before constructing the wooden support for the full-size statue in clay. Note the vernier caliper at the base of the wooden support, used by the sculptor in translating the scale from the small statues to the full-size statue.

The wooden support was then covered in clay and the sculptor carefully constructed the complete anatomy of Colonel Knowlton. All would be soon covered with a skin of clay and then one of clothes, but this meticulous attention to detail was essential for the completed sculpture to be realistic and lifelike.

Sculptor Woods inspected the completed body of Colonel Knowlton, and made refinements before dressing the figure.

Col. Thomas Knowlton of Ashford was one of Connecticut's great Revolutionary War heroes. As a boy he served in the French and Indian War, the siege and capture of Havana in 1762, and was the commander of the Connecticut troops at the Battle of Bunker Hill. He died at the Battle of Harlem Heights on September 16, 1776, at the age of thirty-six.

In 1893, the General Assembly of Connecticut commissioned Mr. E.S. Woods of Hartford to create a statue of Colonel Knowlton after the likeness of him in Trumbull's painting of the Battle of Bunker Hill. The sculptor made several small models of the proposed statue and then made a full-size statue of clay, which was then cast in plaster. Then the mold was made for the final casting in bronze. The completed statue, which stands at the southeast corner of the Capitol, was dedicated on November 13, 1895.

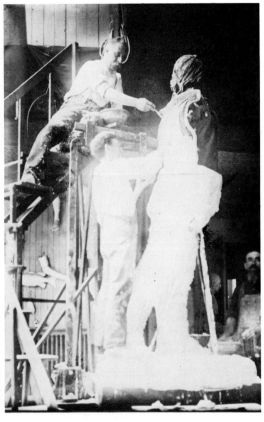

The sculptor then applied the proper britches to the figure. At the base of the statue is the miniature version of the proposed completed work which Woods used as a guide.

This is the completed statue in clay.

Workmen carefully applied plaster to the clay statue in order to create a mold from which the final bronze statue was cast.

The completed bronze statue of Colonel Knowlton stands in the sculptor's studio. The statue on its granite pedestal stands 16'4" high.

Statue of Lafayette

The decision to erect a statue in honor of Marquis de Lafayette seemed a simple one, yet the delays and even the placement of the statue in 1932 and its recent rearrangement have been fraught with discussion and controversy. When the sculptor, Paul Wayland Bartlett, presented the state of Connecticut with the plaster cast of his statue of Lafayette in 1909, it was assumed the sculptor intended the state to have a bronze copy of the statue made. For four years nothing happened. In 1913 it was decided to put up the plaster cast of the statue in the capitol, and this was done with the supervision of Mr. Bartlett. In 1931, Mrs. Frances H. Storrs proposed to have a bronze copy of the statue cast, and have it placed at the intersection of Capitol Avenue and Washington Street. All seemed well until the widow of the sculptor claimed under copyright law that she should supervise the erection of the statue for a fee not to exceed three thousand dollars. In a memo to Judge Burrows the opinion was to not honor Mrs. Bartlett's claim and proceed with the work.

When the various matters were resolved the matter of exactly where to place the statue came up. Around 1931 a wooden facsimile of the proposed statue was constructed, placed on wheels, and then positioned around Lafayette Circle to determine the best location.

It is said that the sculptor, having taken so long to deliver the promised plaster cast of the statue, included a small turtle beside the horse's left hind foot. Fact or fiction, the turtle is indeed part of the completed bronze statue. The statue was cast at the Roman Bronze Works. The granite pedestal was designed by George Keller and erected in ten days by John Russell Deacon. Finally, on November 11, 1932, the generous gift from Mrs. Storrs was unveiled in a public ceremony.

This is the funeral procession of Gov. George L. Lilley, who died in office on April 21, 1909. He was succeeded by Frank B. Weeks. Escorting the hearse are members of the First Company, Governor's Foot Guard, wearing their traditional uniforms. They are the oldest military organization in existence in the country, having been authorized in 1771 to escort and protect the governor of the State of Connecticut.

Main Street

At the corner of Main and Park streets, C.H. Strong carried everything from groceries to used furniture. The scale in front was used to weigh loads of hay brought in from the South End by farmers.

This is Mr. Ellery Hill's, also Mr. Ira Peck's, house on the east side of Main Street. This house has been a private home, a pastoral residence, and today has been converted into offices. Unfortunately its neighbors to the immediate north have been razed.

Next to the Hill-Peck house stood Mrs. Harry Redfield's house.

Mr. David Clark's house on Main Street stood just north of the Redfield's.

Called by some, "the house that wouldn't die," it was built of Windsor brick in 1788-89 by Amos Bull. At that time, most of the some 250 houses in Hartford were of wood. One biographical note on Mr. Bull is that he had five wives: two died, two he divorced, and the last survived him. When the house was completed, Bull used the front room on the first floor to sell linens, hardware, and household items. He sold the house in 1821, and it went through several

hands before 1887 when John C. McManus rented the building. McManus was a local tinsmith and leased the first floor for a stove store.

In 1940 the building, which stood on Main Street near the corner of Charter Oak Avenue, was slated for demolition. Capitol Motors bought the lot, and for financial reasons found it cheaper to move the Bull House to the rear, rather than demolish it. In 1966, as part of urban renewal, the city of Hartford

bought the site and again the Bull House was threatened. The newly formed Connecticut Historical Commission made saving the house an early project. In 1968 Miss Frances A. McCook gave a portion of her home lot on Prospect Street as a new site. In 1971-72 the Bull House was moved to Prospect where it today serves as the headquarters for the Historical Commission.

The Butler-McCook Homestead is the last eighteenth century residential dwelling surviving on Main Street. Built in 1782 by Daniel Butler, a physician and paper manufacturer, it was later owned by the McCook family. Though remodeled through the years, the house was given to the Antiquarian and Landmarks Society of Connecticut by Miss Frances McCook, and is open to the public. Antiquarian and Landmarks has done so much to preserve our rich Connecticut heritage, and a visit to all their properties is more than worthwhile.

This shows the west side of Main, between Capitol and Elm streets. Just to the left of Capitol, stands the 1875 Hotel Capitol. Built for James Welles, whose home once stood there, it has been recently restored to its original grandeur. To the north stands the 1895 Brown Building, and The Linden, which was erected in 1891 as "The Linden, Brown, Thomson & Co.'s Apartment House." It was designed by F.S. Newman of Springfield.

Main Street

At 430 Main stood this wonderful eighteenth century house, converted for commercial use by Lappen and Gordon Company to sell stoves and furnaces.

At the corner of Grove Street, on the left, facing Main stood the elegant Dr. P.W. Ellsworth House. The house next door is missing its chimney and its windows, and since there does not seem to have been a fire, one presumes it is being razed for the new Aetna Life Insurance Building. Today the entire block has been razed and is now part of the Travelers' Tower Square complex.

The buildings on the left, looking north on Main Street, are now replaced by the Gold Building. The wonderful sculpturesque pile is the old Hartford National Bank building on the corner of Main and Pearl. Far up the street Cheney Building's tower can be seen.

The Putnam Phalanax Armory is decorated for an occasion. This block is now the Gold Building, on Main Street.

On Main Street, between Central Row and Grove Street stood the early Wyllys House. When photographed here it had long since ceased functioning as the wonderful private home it had been built to be. Instead it advertises "Uneeda Biscuit," a product of the National Biscuit Company.

Main Street

Main Street, near Pearl, is seen here on the occasion of the visit of the Twenty Mule Borax Team from Death Valley. Boston Branch Grocery was a staple in Hartford for many years.

Top:
Exchange Corner on the east side of Main Street, north of State, is pictured on January 30, 1904, but any viewer could guess it is winter by the dress and swiftness of the pedestrian's movements.

The jewelry store, Hansel Sloan, has just suffered a disastrous fire on Main Street, the corner of Kinsley, where Sage Allen's now stands. The date is 1906.

Market Street

Most people associated the great Cheney Silk Mill with Manchester or with the Cheney Building, now called The Richardson on Main Street. At the corner of Market and Morgan streets the Cheney Company also had this Hartford mill.

This photograph, taken September 19, 1904, shows the mix of single dwellings with commercial establishments along Market Street, from Talcott down to State Street to the south. At the end is the American Hotel, on American Row, today the site of the boat-shaped Phoenix Mutual.

On Market Street, between Kinsley and Temple, stood the Hartford City Hall. It served the city until 1879 when the city moved into the Old State House. This building later served as the Police Court. Today, this site is a parking lot.

It's a Sunday morning, and all is quiet on Market Street south from Temple, April 22, 1906. The loudest thing in sight is the Manchester House's wall board and the Aetna Brewing sign.

Market Street

Rogers Company, a premier company in plated silverware, is on the left on Market Street, south of Kinsley. The other buildings on the left are now occupied by the Connecticut Bank and Trust Company. Various attractions being advertised include Poli's featuring a Hungarian Boys Band, S. Jona and Company Cafe, and a Palm Garden.

This is a timely view from Market Street. Taken in July of 1985, it was but for a moment. The old buildings have been demolished and the new super plaza has yet to block this vista of Central Row and the Old State House. The two tall buildings on Central Row that gracefully complement the Old State House are the Morris and O'Connor 1921 Connecticut Trust Building on the right, and the 1927-28 Voorhees Gmelin and Walker Travelers Insurance Building on the left. Just a corner of Smith and Bassette's 1938-39 Marble Pillar block can be seen at the lower left.

The man in the center is presumably there to direct traffic on Market Street looking north from State Street. In the background, at the corner of Kinsley, stood Hartford's Tammany Hall.

One of the loveliest vistas in Hartford is from the Phoenix Mutual on American Row. Overlooking the sculpture garden, one sees Colt's Dome in the far background.

Morgan Street

Today Morgan Street, what remains of it, is that infernal traffic disaster one must cope with if trying to get onto I-91 north. This April 22, 1906 photograph shows Morgan, looking east from Main Street, down to the Connecticut. Note the gentleman on the left who seems captivated by the advertising poster.

This is the same view, today.

This view of Morgan Street, looking west to Main from Market Street, shows horses and trolleys, kids with bikes, and the building on the left corner advertising the "Socialist, Educational and Political Club."

The foot of Morgan Street, looking back to Main, is seen on August 21, 1903. It is a Friday morning, probably around 10 A.M. The Chicago Dressed Beef warehouse also served as the "East Side Workingmen Club."

The merchants seen here on the south side of Morgan Street, west of Front Street, have banded together to produce one of Hartford's first mall concepts in retailing: "Ladies and Gents, Dry Goods, Infants, Tobacco, Cigars, Cold Soda, Fruit, Candy, Matches, Paper bags, etc." This was taken on November 23, 1906.

North Main Street

Today, to get to North Main Street is a major venture. At the time of this picture, one simply went down the street. The highway built in the 1960s has become a demarcation line, to all of our detriments. North of Morgan one sees the spire of the Fourth Congregational Church and, beyond, North Main Street.

The dry goods store of Keney and Roberts was on North Main Street.

This is the original Keney Homestead and beside it the erection of the Gothic-styled Keney Clock Tower. The tower was a gift to the city, in addition to Keney Park. Philip Goodwin, in *Roof-trees*, said of the tower that it was a lung for a busy city to breathe by, an oasis in the sun. Erected in 1898 by Henry Keney, the plaque on the tower reads: "Erected to the Memory of My Mother." It is said to be the first monument erected in America to a "woman in common life."

This mansion on North Main Street belonged to the Ely family.

The original jail for Hartford stood on Meeting House Square. Later it was moved to the corner of Pearl and Ford streets where the Y.M.C.A. now stands. In 1873 this High Victorian Gothic-styled jail was built on Seyms Street, off North Main. It was designed by George Keller and survived until 1978 when it was demolished.

109

Old State House

Horses queued up where cars and buses do today by the Old State House and its wonderful east lawn. Traditions die hard in Hartford as does a shift in the focus of the city. Then, as now, the central axis is the Old State House. Built in 1796, believed to have been designed by Charles Bulfinch, it sits as a Greek temple atop the hill. Its cupola has inspired many towering landmarks, including the top of the Aetna, West Middle School, and West Hartford's City Hall, to name a few. Threatened with demolition many times, the Old State House survives because people care.

When the Connecticut voters elected Hartford as the sole capital city, the governmental leaders made three decisions: to erect a new monument in Bushnell Park, to sell the Old State House to the city, and to sell the great east lawn to the federal government for the erection of a post office. Here is the Old State House as City Hall in 1900. The building was painted the mayor's favorite color scheme, mustard yellow and dung brown. The Post Office was demolished in 1934.

The Old State House and Meeting House Square have served since the founding of Hartford, and continue to serve as the place where speakers speak, candidates campaign, and things happen. On the Main Street side, the Honorable James G. Blaine from Maine campaigns before a full crowd.

The Old State House is seen as it is today. Behind it is the Connecticut National Bank Building at 799 Main Street, built in 1965-67 and designed by Welton Becket and Associates of New York.

The Old State House continues to preside over the changing landscape. Under construction is Richard Gordon's great Plaza.

Parades on Main Street

Main Street, looking north, is seen decorated with a ceremonial arch. These arches were made of metal and cantilevered to easily span the broad avenue on any occasion. The buildings just to the south of Center Church were razed in 1900, so this photograph predates that.

This is the Ascension Day Parade of the Knights Templars on Main Street. The cupola of the Old State House can just be seen peaking over the buildings.

Parades today seem to run south to north versus north to south. In the old days, having the wind at one's back and not ripping at one's face was preferable when parading down Main Street.

A Veteran's parade troops up Main Street, flag held high.

Parades on Main Street

This parade is moving down Main Street from Centinel Hill, the high point on Main Street where the guards or lookouts were posted in the early days of the colony. Today, G. Fox and Company and WTIC-TV 61 hold the site. The brownstone church is at the corner of Main and Talcott. The brownstone arches of Richardson's Cheney Building can be seen on the right, followed by Fox's, then little more than a hole in the wall. It would take a fire to promote Fox's to the bigness it enjoys today. That, and the distinguished leadership of the incredible Beatrice Fox Auerbach.

Park Central Hotel—Boiler Explosion

Boiler explosions were not an uncommon event, though rarely did one present the photographic image seen here. On February 18, 1889, Hartford's Park Central Hotel at 54 High Street suffered from a boiler explosion. Twenty-two persons were killed in the disaster that destroyed the fifteen-year-old establishment. The photo also presents a clear view of how hotels of the day were furnished: ingrain carpets, upholstered furniture, chests of drawers, sinks, and even electricity.

Park River

The Park or Hog or Meandering Swine river, called in Colonial times the "Little River" is now a buried treasure in Hartford. Because of the devastation wrought by the 1936 and 1938 floods, the river was subsequently banished, and parklets and highways placed on top.

This photograph was taken from the Main Street arched bridge, looking east toward the Connecticut River.

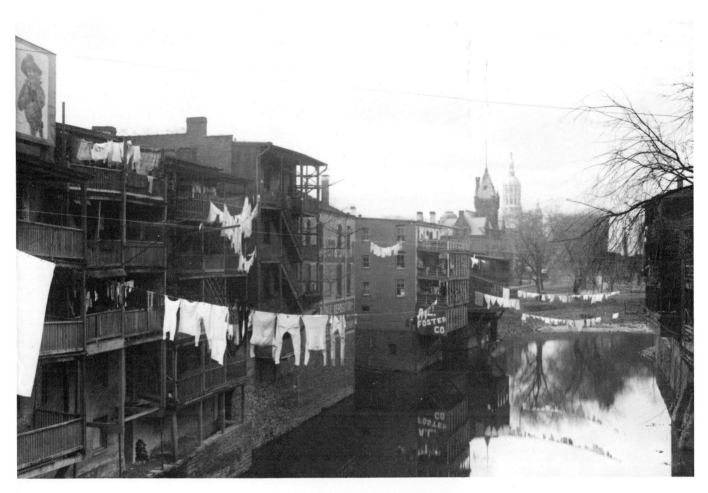

Looking west toward the capitol, one can see the lines for drying clothes stretching across the river.

Pearl Street

The Old Pearl Street Congregational Church stood where Old Bank Lane behind Connecticut National (nee Hartford National) Bank stands. This shot was taken from the roof diagonally across the street on Central Row.

Ministers of the Old Pearl Street Church included the Rev. William DeLoss Love. He wrote *The Colonial History of Hartford* which remains one of the most readable and informative early histories of the city.

The toppling of the steeple of the Old Pearl Street Congregational Church was a spectator's and photographer's delight.

The Phoenix Insurance Company built and moved into this building at 64 Pearl Street in November of 1873.

Pearl Street between Lewis and Main Streets is occupied today by the "Gold Building," One Financial Plaza and its parking garage. The wonderful State Savings Bank with its beehive over the entrance was presumably symbolic of the kind of thrifty worker who saved here. State Savings is now a part of People's Bank and is still located on Pearl Street.

Pearl Street

This was the National Fire Insurance Company's building at the corner of Pearl and Lewis streets. In 1941 they moved to 1000 Asylum Avenue, to the "Collins Compound," their new headquarters designed by Eggers and Higgins of New York. Today that building is the E. Clayton Gengras Medical Center.

The African Methodist Episcopal Zions Church was erected on the corner of Pearl and Ann streets in 1857. Today it is the site of Smith and Bassette's 1926 Hartford Fire Station.

Near the corner of Pearl Street, on Ford Street, stood the Wyman J. May Store. Probably a house converted for the purpose, it appears to be a hardware store, featuring brooms and rope and other household items.

Phoenix Bank

The Phoenix Bank was the second bank in Hartford. Across from the Old State House this building was erected on Main Street. The lions that flank the building have been survivors, and today they grace the Arch Street entrance of City Hall. The rostrum entrance also served as a speaker's platform, and the great orators of the day, including Stephen Douglas spoke here. Erected in 1817, it was Hartford's first marble building.

This is the second Phoenix Bank Building, with the State Bank on the left. The wooden Phoenix has been replaced by one of stone.

This is the third Phoenix Bank Building at the same Main Street location. State Bank, as the Phoenix, has grown, and reflects that growth with a larger, more impressive edifice.

Poverty

The Connecticut Women's Suffrage
Association conducted a vice and
poverty campaign on the streets of
Hartford. Their aim was to record the
impoverished conditions of many who
lived in Hartford ethnic neighborhoods.
We do not know the dates of these
photographs or the exact locations. The
photographer had a grace with the lens
that belies the obviously meager
conditions.

Poverty

Poverty

Poverty

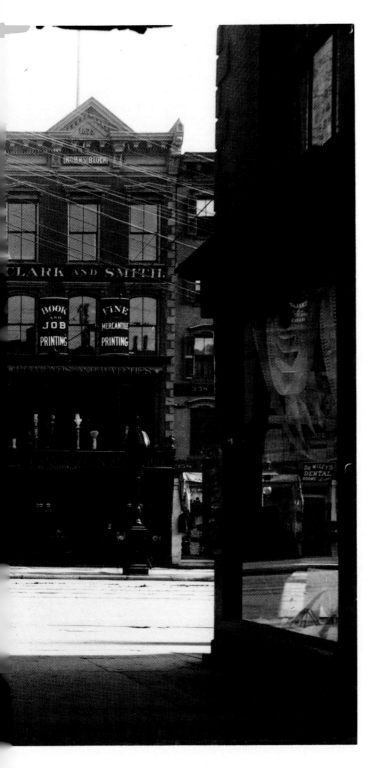

In 1898, the Hart building was razed and replaced by Isaac A. Allen's new building for Charles R. Hart, today known as Sage Allen. The bunting and festooning appear to be in memory of President McKinley. One hopes that the company will someday restore the original street level grandeur of this once elegant facade.

In the 1640 map of the city of Hartford, lot 54 is registered to John Pratt and in this lot he established a farm. Years later his descendants gave part of Pratt's original parcel to the city for the purpose of a road and that road was named in his honor. Today, Pratt Street is a wonderfully busy commercial street.

This is a turn of the century photograph of the Charles R. Hart and Company building looking from Pratt to Main. The shadowy image in the street is a child who couldn't stand still for the timed exposure.

Prospect Street

Prospect Street was originally set out as Meeting House Alley. It connected the homes of the Rev. Thomas Hooker and the first governor, John Haynes, by the Park River with the Meeting House square. The old *Hartford Times* Building now occupies the site of Hooker's house.

Mr. Taylor took this photograph and titled it a "very old house in the rear of east side of Prospect."

The elegant George M. Bartholomew House was at the crest of Prospect Street, west side. The Morgan Memorial of the Wadsworth Atheneum and the Burr Mall now occupy this site.

Prospect Street

Mrs. George Perkins's house was on Prospect Street, west side near the corner of Atheneum Square North. This house was demolished and the Wadsworth Barn moved to create the present domed entrance to the Travelers Insurance Company. Stand on the steps of the Hartford Club and look across at the view and pause.

This is the Elizur Goodrich and Thomas Day house on Prospect Street.

The Connecticut Fire Insurance Building stood on the corner of Prospect and Grove Streets.

Prospect Street

At the corner of Grove and Columbus, near Prospect Street, stands a very small building which houses a local folk hero, "the Chicken Man." A hero because in the best sense of Connecticut independence, when the mighty Travellers Insurance Company offered to buy him out he decided not to sell. When the city threatened to widen the street to handle all the traffic, he took them to court and won. It may be illogically frustrating to the corporations and the politicans, but "the Chicken Man" represents the very motto that founded Hartford: "All power belongs to the people, and only the governed have the right to govern themselves."

In 1873 the Travelers Insurance Company moved into this building on Prospect Street.

On April 1, 1895, H.C. Parsons opened his new Parsons' Theatre on the corner of Prospect and Central Row, east side. The theatre was a mainstay for the theatrical east, and continued in operation until 1936. At the corner of Prospect, American Row, and Central Row, east side, there is a plaque set in the sidewalk marking the site of the old Parsons' Theatre, set by the "New Parsons' Theatre," on the day of its opening: November 1, 1951. It too is now but a distant memory.

In the basement of the Parsons' Theatre was this saloon for refreshments. It was clearly an all men's territory.

Prospect Street

Across the street from the Parsons' Theatre on Prospect stood the Ramsey and later the Dr. Roderic Morrison house. Note the flowering horse chestnuts.

Railroad Round House

From the lantern of the dome of the State Capitol, one was afforded this view of the Railroad Round House in the 1880s. The tracks lead east into Union Station. The great towers in the distance are of the Hartford Public High School on Hopkins Street. It was demolished to make way for Interstate 84. Having decided to level the high school for the highway, and needing a site for a new high school, Hartford's city fathers selected the city's only literary landmark community, the homes of Charles Dudley Warner, William Gillette, Mark Twain, and Harriet Beecher Stowe, and leveled all but the Twain and Stowe houses. In the far upper left can be seen the steeple of the Asylum Hill Congregational Church.

Railroad Round House

On July 8, 1905, locomotive No. 321 ran through the wall of the Hartford Round House leaving this impressive hole. The Round House was later demolished and replaced in 1909 by the State Armory, designed by Benjamin Wistar Morris of New York.

Workmen are digging by hand the new foundation for the new State Armory on the site of the old train Round House. In the left photograph, in the center, is a field john, and behind it the towers of the high school. The house on the hill once belonged to poetess Lydia Sigourney, for whom Sigourney Street is named. In the companion right photo, the work horses are dragging the stones, while in the middle center a train comes round the bend from Union Station.

St. John's Episcopal Church

This is Main Street, looking north, between Linden Place and Elm Street. Mark Twain said Hartford "had the straightest streets that ever led a sinner to destruction." The church in the center is Saint John's Episcopal.

Saint John's Episcopal Church
dominates Main Street in this
photograph taken from Arch Street,
looking north. The towers of the
Wadsworth Atheneum can be seen to the
north. The distinguished Episcopal
clergyman and later Bishop, Arthur

Cleveland Coxe was the first minister of
St. John's. When the Wadsworth
Atheneum was in need of a new wing, in
the early 1900s, J.P. Morgan offered to
purchase the site from St. John's. The
parish accepted and relocated to its
present site on Farmington Avenue.

St. John's Episcopal Church

This is Main Street with old Saint John's, and to the south is the site of the present city hall. It was a functional block, featuring a restaurant, a stable, caskets, plumbing and a laundry. One wonders if the present occupants are as mindful that their business is dependent on their ability to deliver services.

These buildings stood directly south from St. John's, now the Atheneum's Morgan Memorial on Main Street. The wonderful house on the corner of Arch Street is a laundry advertising "High Grade Work, Quick Service, Try Us." Next door, a blacksmith shop, testifying to the number of horses in the town, and just beyond, the original Poli's Theatre. On this site would be erected a grand Poli's Theatre, full of marble staircases and crystal chandeliers, a fantasy to any child, and unfortunately easy prey to every developer. As a child the ambiance of the movie theatre, especially Poli's, was almost as good as the show one went to see.

This view is looking south on Main Street, between Mulberry and Gold streets. The snappy vehicle on the right is a Stevens Duryea, 1902-4. The Poli's Theatre sign is evident on the right, as is The Hartford Market Co.

South Green

South Green and the Methodist Episcopal Church are seen at the southern foot of Main Street. The church today is the South Park Inn, aiding the homeless and the disadvantaged. Its success is largely due to radio personality Brad Davis of WDRC and countless volunteers.

South Green is on the right in this view looking south on Main to Wethersfiled Avenue. The Henry Barnard house is on the left.

Henry Barnard's house on Main Street is opposite South Green. Barnard was one of the state's most distinguished educators, and served as the first commissioner of education from 1867 to 1870. His philosophy of education was "schools good enough for the best and cheap enough for the poorest." Remarkably, the house still stands.

State Arsenal

The State Arsenal was constructed in 1805 at 264 Windsor Avenue in Hartford. Complete with barracks and drilling shed, the site was where the state's munitions were stored.

State Street

The Post Office which was demolished in 1934 occupies the Old State House's east lawn on State Street looking east from Main, circa 1910.

Originally titled "Meeting House to the Landing," State Street once was a premier access road, linking the commerce of the river with the commerce of the city. Most of the buildings on this busy street have been razed, and the sites rebuilt. Two survivors are the Old State House and the 1897-99 First National Bank, today popularly known as the Hartford Federal Savings or Northeast Plaza. Designed by Ernest Flagg of New York it is in the Beaux Arts tradition. Today, though its companions have been demolished to make way for a super shopping and office complex, the building survives, thankfully.

On July 2, 1921, State Street was besieged by over four thousand men and boys who crowded near the *Hartford Courant's* offices to hear the results of the Dempsey-Carpenter fight. The only female present appears to be fleeing the scene (lower right).

On State Street in the 1890s was the Hartford Bank, on the right, and then the great United States Hotel, one of the finest hotels in the city. Honiss's Oyster House opened for business in its basement in 1845, and though substantially changed, the name of the restaurant continues in Hartford today.

In 1872, when the state decided to have one capital, and to build a new building in Bushnell Park, it also decided to let the city of Hartford have the Old State House and to sell the great east lawn to the federal government for the erection of a post office. Construction on the building began in 1873 and was completed in 1883. For years the Post Office was overcrowded and to gain more space threatened the Old State House with demolition. Finally, in 1934 the Post Office was demolished. This view is from State Street looking west to Main.

State Street

This was State Street at the intersection with Front Street, looking west to Main, April 1, 1906. Children play and pose and Poli's advertises Rose Wentworth.

This was the north side of State Street, looking east from Front, November 25, 1906. D.G. Stoughton's Drugstore is on the corner and Tulin, Toft and Tulin promote "the only perfect family flour."

This gathering of men and horses was at the intersection of State and Commerce streets.

State Street

At the foot of State Street, the steam boat *Capitol City* is docked. A principle boat on the Connecticut, it was the last riverboat to pilot the river and stopped service in 1931. Many still remember getting on the *Capitol City* on a Friday night after work and waking up in New York City. For one who has only known the river in the context of highways and the mighty dike, it is incredible that not so long ago one could walk down State Street to the river. The steeple of South Church is seen in the background.

This picture of the south side of State Street on July 10, 1908, shows the tobacco exchanges, and C.H. Talcott and Company which advertises above its front door, "the Naples Formula" and "Peruvian Guano Company." Beyond, cafes advertise beers and lagers and the little bridge and the Connecticut River appear.

Talcott Street

Just north of Fox's stands Talcott Street, so named for the house that Samuel Talcott built there in 1770. In its day it was a grand mansion, and the original home of the famed Talcott settle that William L. Warren presented to the Connecticut Historical Society.

Around 1910, just prior to the demolition of the building, the latter photograph was taken. There is now nothing of its original lines or grace that survives.

Talcott Street, looking east from Main, runs down to the Connecticut River.

Arlington House was best known as St. John's Hotel. Its stables and hitching sheds were used by farmers driving from "over East." It stood on the west side of Main Street, across from Talcott Street. The spire in the right background belongs to the Fourth Congregational Church on North Main Street.

Trumbull Street

Temple Street, which runs just south of the Cheney Building, is now a mere memory of this quick back street that afforded the seasoned traveler a short cut out of Main Street traffic. This is the corner of Main and Temple as it looked April 22, 1906.

In the late 1970s an enclosed walkway was created to protect pedestrians from walking from Sage Allen's to The Richardson. Called Temple Court, it is in the background.

The Cheney Building's tower is on the
right in this view of Temple Street
looking up to Main Street.

Travelers Tower

Since its completion in July of 1919 the Travelers Insurance Company Tower has been and continues to be the dominant beacon on the Hartford skyline. Others may be taller, but none have the personal finesse that this tower has. At some date the top lantern to the tower, shown here, was replaced by its present squattier version. The wonderful brilliance of the golden balls survive, and in the noon sun are a delight to behold. This photo is pre-1934 for the Post Office still occupies the Old State House's east lawn, and the statue of *Justice* still faces Main Street. Only after the Post Office was demolished was *Justice* returned to face east, as she was originally designed to do.

Hartford's County Court House stood at the corner of Trumbull and Allyn streets. Completed in 1885, it served the county until the new court building was erected on Washington Street. In the 1930s it was razed.

The Davis House stood at the corner of Trumbull and Allyn streets. Several notable houses of the period once featured wrought iron railings and balconies like these shown here. The Civic Center now dominates this site.

Trumbull Street

The John Corning residence stood back of the Hall of Records on Trumbull, at the corner of Pearl. The Corning Fountain is named for this family.

This detail of the door of the Corning residence was taken after the family had left. The signs note the changing times, from private dwelling to "Furnished Rooms, Transients Accommodated."

The wonderful Hartford Insurance Company stood at the corner of Trumball and Pearl streets. Today, the new City Place is on this site.

These ruins are of the old buildings in the rear of Case, Lockwood, and Brainard press, today Connecticut Printers. They were rumored to be the 1720 Meeting House that burned and was replaced by today's Old State House. Stories tell of the remaining meeting house being moved first to Church Street and then to this site off Trumbull. If true, it appears to be the right hand wing of the building presented. Hopefully someday a full excavation of the west side of the Old State House property will be conducted. Beneath the bricks one will probably find the original foundations of both the seventeenth century Meeting House and of the 1720 structure. If Franklin's home in Philadelphia could be recovered, Meeting House Square is a natural. Lets fund a dig to recover Old Hartford.

At the foot of Trumbull Street, where the phone company building now stands, once stood the monumental factories of Jewell Belting Company. Pliny (pronounced as in *slimy* in Hartford, as in *skinny* in Boston) Jewell was descended from a family of tanners. In 1826 he conceived of making belting out of leather, of a sufficient quality and durability to be substituted for gears in transmitting water and steam power to machines. In 1845, Jewell built these factories beside the Park River. In many old photographs the letters "Jewell Belting Company" dot the horizon. Jewell Street is named for the man whose factories dominated the scene.

Underwood Typewriter

The Underwood Typewriter Factory operated in Hartford for many years, and had a great complex on Arbor Street. How this picture came to be taken is not known, but surely this man's dedication to his Underwood, and his Underwood's ability to stand the heat deserve notice. It may be the simple fact that the heating company has unjustly cut off the heat, all bottles of ink have frozen solid, and the man's only recourse is to write in protest, on his Underwood.

Lydia Huntley Sigourney was "The Sweet Singer of Hartford." This house was built for her in 1820 by her husband Charles Sigourney, a Hartford merchant. Originally, the house overlooked spacious gardens and the little river. With the advent of the railroad, much of the land was taken for the iron horse. Mrs. Sigourney found the train noisey, dirty and wrote: "The iron horse has since tramped over these premises, annihilated the grove...and with his fiery breath consumed an ancient pair of elms." The mansion was demolished in 1938.

Union Station

An early magazine engraving shows the original Union Station, and on the hill Mrs. Sigourney's house. The river shown at the right is the Park or Hog or Meandering Swine River that once flowed around and through Bushnell Park and on to the Connecticut River. It is curious that the artist has shown pedestrians walking along the tracks, especially as the grade level crossing at Asylum Street was of great concern and eventually resulted in the construction of a new station with safe above grade tracks.

Union Station

In the 1840s the railroad was here to stay, and many cities began erecting proper stations to handle both passengers and the goods the iron horse brought. The first station in Hartford was built in 1849, at the corner of Union Place and Asylum Street, where the present station now stands. This wonderful Italianate structure had grade level depot, as can be seen with No. 10 awaiting to depart. Concerned that trains might collide with pedestrians or with carriages, the State Board of Railroad Commissioners decided to alter the grade, thus rendering this station obsolete. Hartford architect George Keller drew up the plans that created the grade known today when entering Hartford by train.

The present Union Station was built in 1887-89, and designed by Shepley Rutan and Coolidge of Boston. Unlike its predecessor this station faces Union Place and not Bushnell Park. In 1914 a fire broke out that greatly altered the central portion of the building. Horse-drawn sleds contained the hoses used for fighting the fire in sub-zero weather. The original entrance of the building, with its great gables can be seen in the middle right. Following the fire the walls were extended to provide a full second floor.

To the northeast of the actual station near the river lay the complex system of tracks and switchings comprising the old freight yard. This view of the yard was taken on September 3, 1903, looking south.

Wadsworth Atheneum

This is the Jeremiah Wadsworth House which once stood on the site of the Wadsworth Atheneum. This house was moved in 1842 to Buckingham Street and then demolished in 1887.

In 1842 the Wadsworth Atheneum was founded. Its original building on Main Street was the work of Henry Austin who studied under Ithiel Town of New Haven. In front of the building stands the Wadsworth Elm Tree, where Washington, Rochambeau and Wadsworth conferred. Later street improvements have drastically lowered the level of Main Street, so it is no longer just a gentle slope and a few steps to the main entrance. Note the stained glass over the entrance and the fact that beside the front door the windows are indicated but not installed.

For the fiftieth anniversary of the
Wadsworth Atheneum the trustees voted
to improve the original building. Shown
here are some of the changes, including
the installation of clear glass above the
main door, and the installation of
windows beside it.

Wadsworth Atheneum

With the encouragement of his cousin the Rev. Francis Goodwin, J.P. Morgan donated the Morgan Memorial to the Wadsworth Atheneum. Shown here is the laying of the cornerstone for the Morgan Memorial. The Reverend Goodwin is the gentleman with the trowel. The date is April 23, 1908. Of all our citizens, the Rev. Francis Goodwin did as much as any to affect positive change for, and in, our city. As the rector of Trinity Church he abolished the practice of renting pews. As an amateur architect he helped design his father's house on Woodland Street, known as Goodwin Castle. He was a mainstay of the Atheneum and other civic causes. His greatest legacy is without doubt the Hartford Park system. Following Horace Bushnell's lead and example, Pope, Elizabeth, and Keeney parks were set aside for all to enjoy. Goodwin Park is appropriately named in his honor.

The occasion seen here on Main Street, at the corner of Atheneum Square North, is the reunion of the Hartfc Wheel Club's start for Fenwick, a' mouth of the Connecticut River September 19-20, 1914.

This view is looking south or n Street from Grove to Athene: quare North. Today this belongs t e Travelers.

Washington Street

When Mark Twain first visited Hartford in 1868, he wrote back to his readers in California that in Hartford the homes are "massive private hotels. Each house sits on an acre of green grass, or trees...." Washington Street in Hartford may well have been the street that so impressed Twain, and indeed its stately dwellings, even when preserved in photographs, are a wonder.

Washington Street is seen looking south. In the winter this great thoroughfare was notorious for its day and midnight sleigh races.

The residence of Gen. Lucius A. Barbour is seen on the right in this view of Washington Street looking north. It is one of the few survivors of all the great homes that once held the street.

Washington Street

On the west side of Washington, where the Court House now stands, once stood Mr. Morgan B. Brainard's house, top; Mr. Kelso Davis's house, middle; and Mrs. Leverett Brainard's house, bottom. It is curious that a financially and politically powerful group had their home sites chosen for the new Court House. Chance or the opportunity to leave a dying neighborhood ahead of the demise?

On the east side of Washington were two singularly special houses: Mrs. Charles Jewell's house with its marvelously castlelated towers, and another, whose entrance once seen one never forgets. It belonged to many families: Pratt; Northan; Lee; and the Misses Taylor, daughters of Mr. Samuel Taylor who took this and so many of these pictures. It was his daughter Mary who presented his original glass negative plates to the State Library in 1957. Now, nearly thirty years later, they have been so well preserved that they have been used to produce many of the photographs presented here.

Wethersfield Avenue

This is the Winshop House, possibly on Wethersfield Avenue. This photograph was taken by Mr. Samuel Taylor, whose superb photographs preserve so much of Hartford. Unfortunately, other than list the name of the house, Mr. Taylor did not provide the address, as he did in so many cases.

The home of Mrs. Mary J. Munsell still stands at the corner of Wyllys Street and Wethersfield Avenue. Mrs. Munsell was the daughter of Gail Borden, the first man to find a good way of making evaporated milk.

Woodland Street

This picture of Woodland Street was taken on Arbor Day. Woodland Street took its name from the great woods surrounding it. In 1954, concurrent with the national celebrations of Arbor Day, the city of Hartford began the widening of Woodland Street. As others were planting trees, the great trees were cut on the street, leaving only the stumps seen on the left.

World War I
Signing Up

When the United States declared war on Germany, Connecticut, and especially Hartford, responded with a complete all out effort. Over sixty-seven thousand Connecticut men went to war.

The corner of Pearl and Main featured a great enlistment banner, "Real Men Wanted." Note the little policeman at the instersection, who is the sole giver of the "Stop" and "Go." On the near right a hay wagon proceeds up Main, followed by a small electric.

These men are lined up for the first draft registration in Hartford. Two trolley cars located at the corner of Main and Morgan streets were used for the registration.

Many young men went to sign up at the Hall of Records, located at the corner of Pearl and Trumbull. It was built in 1853, and served as the Hall of Records until the new City Hall was built in 1915. During the war it was the draft and registration headquarters, then a veterans service club, and finally an office building before it was razed in 1940. Its multiple use is evident even here with the Oriental rug sale being advertised on one side and the millinery sign with its glass showcase of samples on the other.

These draftees posed outside on the
steps of the Hall of Records.

This Army recruiting tent was pitched on the Old State House grounds.

Complete with hats and ties, a Hartford contingent is marching to depart for Camp Devens.

Family members said good-bye to husbands, sons, fathers, and brothers at Hartford's Union Station.

World War I
Departing for Camp Devens

Drafted troops are departing for Camp
Devens in these scenes at the railroad
yard.

World War I "Preparedness"

Maj. Gen. Clarence R. Edwards, commandant of the Twenty-sixth Division was received at Union Station in Hartford.

The First Company Governor's Foot Guard exchanged courtesies with the Black Watch, Canadian regiment under arms. It was the first time the Black Watch had been welcomed in the United States. In this shot taken outside the Union Station, note the buildings on the left, all of which have been demolished, but which once gave Union Place a distinguished profile.

"Preparedness" was the watchword. Here the Connecticut State Guard is on emergency duty, complete with machine gun, in Bushnell Park.

The regular army cavalry, on the move from station to station, is seen here pausing beside the State Armory.

World War I "Preparedness"

Capt. R.M. Yergason was photographed just before the departure of the First Connecticut Ambulance Company for the Mexican border.

A British tank is seen on display in Pope Park. The tank is covered with graffiti, all supportive of the war effort.

A demonstration of the gas mask is given by this man.

Hartford boys are seen in machine gun drill on Poli's Stage.

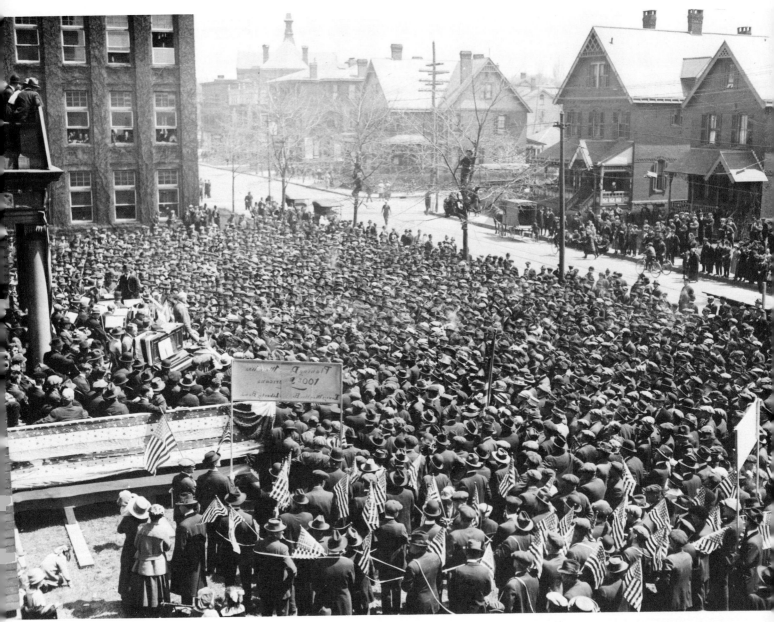

Supporting the war meant more than
sending one's sons or daughters to the
effort. Bandages, clothes, and especially
liberty loans were raised to stop the
enemy.

This is a Liberty Loan rally outside
Pratt and Whitney.

The Old State House, as the center of Hartford, served as a rallying point and a fundraising focus for the war effort.

This Liberty Loan Rally was at the Old State House.

The mayor of Hartford is spinning the barrell in the thrift stamp lottery.

World War I
Supporting the War

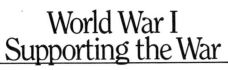

Two indefatigable war workers were Mrs. Morgan G. Bulkeley, left and Mrs. Richard M. Bissell.

Governor Holcomb, Morgan G. Bulkeley, Mrs. Richard M. Bissell, and others are seen outside the Liberty Bond booth at the Old State House.

As the war dragged on, Hartford spirits and determinism did not falter. Instead, a new improved Liberty Cottage was erected at the Old State House to raise more money.

The campaigns were successful, as the banner at the Old State House proclaims: "$250,000; Hartford did it with $10,000 over!"

Mrs. Morgan G. Bulkeley, a determined fundraiser, made sure the recipient of her call got the message and did not fail to give...and then used a softer tone for the photographer. She is seen wearing the epitome of a high style hat.

Girl Red Cross workers from the Hartford
Chapter are seen working on gifts for the
boys overseas.

In the lower level of the City Hall, volunteers held a flower sale to aid the war effort.

This woman was a railroad crossing tender during the war.

Parades were a vital part of public morale. Here the Red Cross Volunteers are seen on parade down Main Street from the Old State House.

Some rode rather than walked, perhaps so the volunteer in the back could finish her knitting while on parade.

The First Company Governor's Foot Guard are seen parading as an escort during a war time parade.

Colt's decorated float was photographed outside the Wadsworth Atheneum in a war time parade.

World War I Patriotic Displays

The Travelers Insurance Company's Main Street building was decorated for the war effort.

Merchants and store keepers participated in the war fever. Here is the patriotic display presented by C.S. Hills and Company.

The banners change at Main Street and
Pearl, but the war drags on. When will it
be over?

World War I
Welcome Home!

The British and American flags fly from the corner of Main and Pearl. The war is over and this is the first Armistice Celebration, November 11, 1918.

The Welcome Home Arch was erected on Asylum Street, just before High and Ford streets. The Hotel Garde is in the background.

This is the first Connecticut soldier home from France. Unfortunately, the records do not preserve his name.

World War I
Welcome Home!

Connecticut's 102nd Infantry Division
returned on April 30, 1919.

Suggested Reading

Many worthy histories of Hartford have been written, and there are some more in the process. If one is interested in reading more about Hartford, I would encourage you to check with your public library, local bookstores, the Old State House's Museum shop and especially the Connecticut Historical Society. The society continues to print first rate publications on Hartford and all of Connecticut. Currently in the works include a new history of the city by Mr. Ellsworth Grant. His wife, Marion Grant, is updating and enlarging her invaluable tour-history of the city. The Connecticut Historical Society also publishes a first rate member's newsletter which could be of interest to all.

The following list is not meant to be a definitive bibliography, but it is rather a few selections that the reader may find interesting:

"The Connecticut Antiquarian," the bulletin of The Antiquarian and Landmarks Society Inc. of Connecticut. Sold separately or is free to members.

My Hartford of the Nineteenth Century. Helen Post Chapman, Hartford, 1928. A delightful short book of memories of old Hartford.

The Colonial History of Hartford. William DeLoss Love, reprinted 1974, Centinel Hill Press.

Hartford, an Illustrated History of Connecticut's Capital. Glen Weaver, Windsor Publications, Inc., 1982. A highly readable and fully illustrated history by one of the areas most prominent historians.

As reference materials, the reader might be interested in the following:

Christopher and Bonnie B. Collier. *The Literature of Connecticut History*, Occasional papers of the Connecticut Humanities Council, No. 6. Middletown, Connecticut Humanities Council, 1983.

Thomas J. Kemp. *Connecticut Researcher's Handbook.* Detroit, Gale Research Company, 1981.

In June of 1986 The Committee for a New England Bibliography will issue *Connecticut: A Bibliography of its History*, compiled by Roger Parks.

About the Author

WILSON H. FAUDE is a graduate of Darrow School, Hobart College and holds a master's degree in American History from Trinity College. He is currently the executive director of the Old State House in Hartford, the former capitol of Connecticut. From 1971 through 1977 he was curator of the Mark Twain House in Hartford. He served as executive director of the Old State House from 1978 through 1981, then as executive associate to the vice-president of development at the University of Hartford until his return to the Old State House in 1985. Mr. Faude has contributed articles to *Winterthur, Antiques* and other periodicals, is the author of *The Renaissance of Mark Twain's House* and co-author with Joan W. Friedland of *Birthplace of Democracy* and *Connecticut Firsts.* Currently, Mr. Faude is a member of the state's 350th Anniversary Committee and chairman of the Connecticut Historical Commission. Mr. Faude lives in West Hartford.